D1360432

COURAGE

THE RECTORIAL ADDRESS
DELIVERED AT ST. ANDREWS UNIVERSITY
MAY 3, 1922

COURAGE

BY
J. M. BARRIE

NEW YORK
CHARLES SCRIBNER'S SONS
1928

TO
THE RED GOWNS OF ST. ANDREWS

COURAGE

YOU have had many rectors here in St. Andrews who will continue in bloom long after the lowly ones such as I am are dead and rotten and forgotten. They are the roses in December; you remember someone said that God gave us memory so that we might have roses in December. But I do not envy the great ones. In my experience—and you may find in the end it is yours also—the people I have cared for most and who have seemed most worth caring for— my December roses—have been very simple folk. Yet I wish that for this hour I could swell into someone of importance, so as to do you credit. I suppose you had a melting for me because I was hewn out of one of your own quarries, walked similar academic groves, and have trudged the road on which you will soon set forth. I would that I could put into your hands a staff for that somewhat bloody march, for though there is much about myself that I conceal from other people, to help you I would expose every cranny of my mind.

But, alas, when the hour strikes for the rector to answer to his call he is unable to become the undergraduate he used to be, and so the only door into you is closed. We, your elders, are much more interested in you than you are in us. We are not really important to you. I have utterly forgotten the address of the rector of my time, and even who he was, but I recall vividly climbing up a statue to tie his colours round its neck and being hurled therefrom with contumely. We remember the important things. I cannot provide you with that staff for your journey; but perhaps I can tell you a little about it, how to use it and lose it and find it again, and cling to it more than ever. You shall cut it —so it is ordained—every one of you for himself, and its name is courage. You must excuse me if I talk a good deal about courage to you to-day. There is nothing else much worth speaking about to undergraduates or graduates or white-haired men and women. It is the lovely virtue—the rib of Himself that God sent down to His children.

My special difficulty is that though you have had literary rectors here before, they were the big guns, the historians, the philosophers; you have had none, I think, who followed my more humble branch, which may be described as playing hide and seek with angels. My puppets seem more real to me than myself, and I could get on much more swingingly if I made one of them deliver

this address. It is M'Connachie who
has brought me to this pass. M'Connachie, I should explain, as I have
undertaken to open the innermost doors,
is the name I give to the unruly half
of myself: the writing half. We are
complement and supplement. I am the
half that is dour and practical and
canny, he is the fanciful half; my desire
is to be the family solicitor, standing
firm on my hearth rug among the harsh
realities of the office furniture; while
he prefers to fly around on one wing.
I should not mind him doing that,
but he drags me with him. I have
sworn that M'Connachie shall not inter-
fere with this address to-day; but
there is no telling. I might have done
things worth while if it had not been for
M'Connachie, and my first piece of advice to you at any rate shall be sound:
don't copy me. A good subject for a rec-

torial address would be the mess the rector himself has made of life. I merely cast this forth as a suggestion, and leave the working of it out to my successor. I do not think it has been used yet.

My own theme is Courage, as you should use it in the great fight that seems to me to be coming between youth and their betters; by youth, meaning, of course, you, and by your betters, us. I want you to take up this position: That youth have for too long left exclusively in our hands the decisions in national matters that are more vital to them than to us. Things about the next war, for instance, and why the last one ever had a beginning. I use the word fight because it must, I think, begin with a challenge; for the aim is the reverse of antagonism, it is partnership. I want you to hold that the time has arrived for youth to demand a partnership, and to demand it courageously. That to gain courage is what you come to St. Andrews for. With some alarums and excursions into college life. That is what I propose, but, of course, the issue lies with M'Connachie.

Your betters had no share in the immediate cause of the war; we know what nation has that blot to wipe out; but for fifty years or so we heeded not the rumblings of the distant drum, I do not mean by lack of military preparations; and when war did come we told youth, who had to get us out of it, tall tales of what it really is and of the clover beds to which it leads. We were not meaning to deceive, most of us were as honourable and as ignorant as the youth themselves; but that does not acquit us of failings such as stupidity and jealousy, the two black spots in human nature which, more than love of money, are at the root of all evil. If you prefer to leave things as they are we shall probably fail you again. Do not be too sure that we have learned our lesson, and are not at this very moment doddering down some brimstone path.

I am far from implying that even worse things than war may not come to a State. There are circumstances in which nothing can so well become a land, as I think this land proved when the late war did break out and there was but one thing to do. There is a form of anæmia that is more rotting than even an unjust war. The end will indeed have come to our courage and to us when we are afraid in dire mischance to refer the final appeal to the arbitrament of arms. I suppose all the lusty of our race, alive and dead, join hands on that.

> " And he is dead who will not fight;
> And who dies fighting has increase."

But if you must be in the struggle, the more reason you should know why, before it begins, and have a say in the decision whether it is to begin. The youth who went to the war had no such knowledge, no such say; I am sure the survivors, of whom there must be a number here to-day, want you to be wiser than they were, and are certainly determined to be wiser next time themselves. If you are to get that partnership, which, once gained, is to be for mutual benefit, it will be, I should say, by banding yourselves with these men, not defiantly but firmly, not for selfish ends but for your country's good. In the meantime they have one bulwark; they have a General who is befriending them as I think never, after the fighting was over, has a General befriended his men before. Perhaps the seemly thing would be for us, their betters, to elect one of these young surviv-

ors of the carnage to be our Rector. He
ought now to know a few things about
war that are worth our hearing. If his
theme were the Rector's favourite, diligence, I should be afraid of his advising
a great many of us to be diligent in sit-
ting still and doing no more harm.

Of course he would put it more suavely
than that, though it is not, I think, by
gentleness that you will get your rights;
we are dogged ones at sticking to what
we have got, and so will you be at our
age. But avoid calling us ugly names;
we may be stubborn and we may be
blunderers, but we love you more than
aught else in the world, and once you
have won your partnership we shall all
be welcoming you. I urge you not to use
ugly names about anyone. In the war
it was not the fighting men who were
distinguished for abuse; as has been well
said, "Hell hath no fury like a non-

combatant." Never ascribe to an opponent motives meaner than your own. There may be students here to-day who have decided this session to go in for immortality, and would like to know of an easy way of accomplishing it. That is a way, but not so easy as you think. Go through life without ever ascribing to your opponents motives meaner than your own. Nothing so lowers the moral currency; give it up, and be great.

Another sure way to fame is to know what you mean. It is a solemn thought that almost no one—if he is truly eminent—knows what he means. Look at the great ones of the earth, the politicians. We do not discuss what they say, but what they may have meant when they said it. In 1922 we are all wondering, and so are they, what they meant in 1914 and afterwards. They are publishing books trying to find out; the men

of action as well as the men of words.
There are exceptions. It is not that our
statesmen are "sugared mouths with
minds therefrae"; many of them are the
best men we have got, upright and anx-
ious, nothing cheaper than to miscall
them. The explanation seems just to be
that it is so difficult to know what you
mean, especially when you have become a
swell. No longer apparently can you deal
in "russet yeas and honest kersey noes";
gone for ever is simplicity, which is as
beautiful as the divine plain face of
Lamb's Miss Kelly. Doubts breed
suspicions, a dangerous air. Without
suspicion there might have been no war.
When you are called to Downing Street
to discuss what you want of your betters
with the Prime Minister he won't be
suspicious, not as far as you can see;
but remember the atmosphere of gen-
erations you are in, and when he passes

you the toast-rack say to yourselves, if you would be in the mode, "Now, I wonder what he meant by that."

Even without striking out in the way I suggest, you are already disturbing your betters considerably. I sometimes talk this over with M'Connachie, with whom, as you may guess, circumstances compel me to pass a good deal of my time. In our talks we agree that we, your betters, constantly find you forgetting that we are your betters. Your answer is that the war and other happenings have shown you that age is not necessarily another name for sapience; that our avoidance of frankness in life and in the arts is often, but not so often as you think, a cowardly way of shirking unpalatable truths, and that you have taken us off our pedestals because we look more natural on the ground. You who are at the rash age even accuse your

elders, sometimes not without justifica-
tion, of being more rash than yourselves.
"If Youth but only knew," we used to
teach you to sing; but now, just because
Youth has been to the war, it wants to
change the next line into "If Age had
only to do."

In so far as this attitude of yours is
merely passive, sullen, negative, as it
mainly is, despairing of our capacity and
anticipating a future of gloom, it is no
game for man or woman. It is certainly
the opposite of that for which I plead.
Do not stand aloof, despising, disbe-
lieving, but come in and help—insist on
coming in and helping. After all, we
have shown a good deal of courage; and
your part is to add a greater courage to
it. There are glorious years lying ahead
of you if you choose to make them glorious. God's in His heaven still. So for-
ward, brave hearts. To what adven-

tures I cannot tell, but I know that your God is watching to see whether you are adventurous. I know that the great partnership is only a first step, but I do not know what are to be the next and the next. The partnership is but a tool; what are you to do with it? Very little, I warn you, if you are merely thinking of yourselves; much if what is at the marrow of your thoughts is a future that even you can scarcely hope to see.

Learn as a beginning how world-shaking situations arise and how they may be countered. Doubt all your betters who would deny you that right of partnership. Begin by doubting all such in high places—except, of course, your professors. But doubt all other professors—yet not conceitedly, as some do, with their noses in the air; avoid all such physical risks. If it necessitates your pushing some of us out of our places, still push; you will find it needs some shoving. But the things courage can do! The things that even incompetence can do if it works with singleness of purpose. The war has done at least one big thing: it has taken spring out of the year. And, this accomplished, our leading people are amazed to find that the other seasons are not conducting themselves as usual. The spring of the year lies buried in the fields of France and elsewhere. By the time the next eruption comes it may be you who are responsible for it and your sons who are in the lava. All, perhaps, because this year you let things slide.

We are a nice and kindly people, but it is already evident that we are stealing back into the old grooves, seeking cushions for our old bones, rather than attempting to build up a fairer future. That is what we mean when we say that the country is settling down. Make haste, or you will become like us, with only the thing we proudly call experience to add to your stock, a poor exchange for the generous feelings that time will take away. We have no intention of giving you your share. Look around and see how much share Youth has now that the war is over. You got a handsome share while it lasted.

I expect we shall beat you; unless your fortitude be doubly girded by a desire to send a message of cheer to your brothers who fell, the only message, I believe, for which they crave; they are not worrying about their Aunt Jane. They want to know if you have learned wisely from what befell them; if you have, they will be braced in the feeling that they did not die in vain. Some of them think they did. They will not take our word for it that they did not. You are their living image; they know you

could not lie to them, but they distrust
our flattery and our cunning faces. To
us they have passed away; but are you
who stepped into their heritage only
yesterday, whose books are scarcely cold
to their hands, you who still hear their
cries being blown across the links—are
you already relegating them to the
shades? The gaps they have left in this
University are among the most honourable of her wounds. But we are not
here to acclaim them. Where they are
now, hero is, I think, a very little word.
They call to you to find out in time the
truth about this great game, which your
elders play for stakes and Youth plays
for its life.

I do not know whether you are grown
a little tired of that word hero, but I am
sure the heroes are. That is the subject
of one of our unfinished plays; M'Connachie is the one who writes the plays.

If any one of you here proposes to be a playwright you can take this for your own and finish it. The scene is a school, schoolmasters present, but if you like you could make it a university, professors present. They are discussing an illuminated scroll about a student fallen in the war, which they have kindly presented to his parents; and unexpectedly the parents enter. They are an old pair, backbent, they have been stalwarts in their day but have now gone small; they are poor, but not so poor that they could not send their boy to college. They are in black, not such a rusty black either, and you may be sure she is the one who knows what to do with his hat. Their faces are gnarled, I suppose—but I do not need to describe that pair to Scottish students. They have come to thank the Senatus for their lovely scroll and to ask them to

tear it up. At first they had been en-
amoured to read of what a scholar their
son was, how noble and adored by all.
But soon a fog settled over them, for
this grand person was not the boy they
knew. He had many a fault well known
to them; he was not always so noble;
as a scholar he did no more than scrape
through; and he sometimes made his
father rage and his mother grieve.
They had liked to talk such memories
as these together, and smile over them,
as if they were bits of him he had left
lying about the house. So thank you
kindly, and would you please give them
back their boy by tearing up the scroll?
I see nothing else for our dramatist to
do. I think he should ask an alumna
of St. Andrews to play the old lady (indicating Miss Ellen Terry). The love-
liest of all young actresses, the dearest
of all old ones; it seems only yesterday

that all the men of imagination proposed to their beloveds in some such frenzied words as these, "As I can't get Miss Terry, may I have you?"

This play might become historical as the opening of your propaganda in the proposed campaign. How to make a practical advance? The League of Nations is a very fine thing, but it cannot save you, because it will be run by us. Beware your betters bringing presents. What is wanted is something run by yourselves. You have more in common with the youth of other lands than Youth and Age can ever have with each other; even the hostile countries sent out many a son very like ours, from the same sort of homes, the same sort of universities, who had as little to do as our youth had with the origin of the great adventure. Can we doubt that many of these on both sides who have gone over and were once opponents are now friends? You ought to have a League of Youth of all countries as your beginning, ready to say to all Governments, "We will fight each other but only when we are sure of the necessity." Are you equal to your job, you young men? If not, I call upon the red-gowned women to lead the way. I sound to myself as if I were advocating a rebellion, though I am really asking for a larger friendship. Perhaps I may be arrested on leaving the hall. In such a cause I should think that I had at last proved myself worthy to be your Rector.

You will have to work harder than ever, but possibly not so much at the same things; more at modern languages certainly if you are to discuss that League of Youth with the students of other nations when they come over to St. Andrews for the Conference. I am

far from taking a side against the classics.
I should as soon argue against your hav-
ing tops to your heads; that way lie
the best tops. Science, too, has at last
come to its own in St. Andrews. It is
the surest means of teaching you how to
know what you mean when you say.
So you will have to work harder. Isaak
Walton quotes the saying that doubtless the Almighty could have created
a finer fruit than the strawberry, but
that doubtless also He never did.
Doubtless also He could have provided
us with better fun than hard work, but
I don't know what it is. To be born
poor is probably the next best thing.
The greatest glory that has ever come
to me was to be swallowed up in Lon-
don, not knowing a soul, with no means
of subsistence, and the fun of working
till the stars went out. To have known
anyone would have spoilt it. I did not

even quite know the language. I rang for my boots, and they thought I said a glass of water, so I drank the water and worked on. There was no food in the cupboard, so I did not need to waste time in eating. The pangs and agonies when no proof came. How courteously tolerant was I of the postman without a proof for us; how M'Connachie, on the other hand, wanted to punch his head. The magic days when our article appeared in an evening paper. The promptitude with which I counted the lines to see how much we should get for it. Then M'Connachie's superb air of dropping it into the gutter. Oh, to be a free lance of journalism again—that darling jade! Those were days. Too good to last. Let us be grave. Here comes a Rector.

But now, on reflection, a dreadful sinking assails me, that this was not

really work. The artistic callings—you
remember how Stevenson thumped them
—are merely doing what you are clam-
orous to be at; it is not real work unless
you would rather be doing something
else. My so-called labours were just
M'Connachie running away with me
again. Still, I have sometimes worked;
for instance, I feel that I am working at
this moment. And the big guns are in
the same plight as the little ones.
Carlyle, the king of all rectors, has
always been accepted as the arch-apostle
of toil, and has registered his many
woes. But it will not do. Despite sick-
ness, poortith, want and all, he was
grinding all his life at the one job he
revelled in. An extraordinarily happy
man, though there is no direct proof that
he thought so.

There must be many men in other
callings besides the arts lauded as hard

workers who are merely out for enjoyment. Our Chancellor? (indicating Lord Haig). If our Chancellor had always a passion to be a soldier, we must reconsider him as a worker. Even our Principal? How about the light that burns in our Principal's room after decent people have gone to bed? If we could climb up and look in—I should like to do something of that kind for the last time—should we find him engaged in honest toil, or guiltily engrossed in chemistry?

You will all fall into one of those two callings, the joyous or the uncongenial; and one wishes you into the first, though our sympathy, our esteem, must go rather to the less fortunate, the braver ones who "turn their necessity to glorious gain" after they have put away their dreams. To the others will go the easy prizes of life—success, which has become a somewhat odious onion now-

adays, chiefly because we so often give
the name to the wrong thing. When
you reach the evening of your days you
will, I think, see—with, I hope, becoming cheerfulness—that we are all
failures, at least all the best of us. The
greatest Scotsman that ever lived wrote
himself down a failure:

> "The poor inhabitant below
> Was quick to learn and wise to know,
> And keenly felt the friendly glow
>   And softer flame.
> But thoughtless follies laid him low.
>   And stained his name."

Perhaps the saddest lines in poetry,
written by a man who could make
things new for the gods themselves.

If you want to avoid being like Burns
there are several possible ways. Thus
you might copy us, as we shine forth
in our published memoirs, practically
without a flaw. No one so obscure
nowadays but that he can have a book

about him. Happy the land that can produce such subjects for the pen.

But do not put your photograph at all ages into your autobiography. That may bring you to the ground. "My Life; and what I have done with it"; that is the sort of title, but it is the photographs that give away what you have done with it. Grim things, those portraits; if you could read the language of them you would often find it unnecessary to read the book. The face itself, of course, is still more tell-tale, for it is the record of all one's past life. There the man stands in the dock, page by page; we ought to be able to see each chapter of him melting into the next like the figures in the cinematograph. Even the youngest of you has got through some chapters already. When you go home for the next vacation some one is sure to say "John has changed a little; I don't quite see in what way, but he has changed." You remember they said that last vacation. Perhaps it means that you look less like your father. Think that out. I could say some nice things of your betters if I chose.

In youth you tend to look rather frequently into a mirror, not at all necessarily from vanity. You say to yourself, "What an interesting face; I wonder what he is to be up to?" Your elders do not look into the mirror so often. We know what he has been up to. As yet there is unfortunately no science of reading other people's faces; I think a chair for this should be founded in St. Andrews.

The new professor will need to be a sublime philosopher, and for obvious reasons he ought to wear spectacles before his senior class. It will be a glori-

ously optimistic chair, for he can tell his
students the glowing truth, that what
their faces are to be like presently de-
pends mainly on themselves. Mainly,
not altogether—

> " I am the master of my fate,
> I am the captain of my soul."

I found the other day an old letter
from Henley that told me of the circumstances in which he wrote that poem.
" I was a patient," he writes, " in the old
infirmary of Edinburgh. I had heard
vaguely of Lister, and went there as a
sort of forlorn hope on the chance of
saving my foot. The great surgeon re-
ceived me, as he did and does everybody,
with the greatest kindness, and for
twenty months I lay in one or other
ward of the old place under his care. It
was a desperate business, but he saved
my foot, and here I am." There he
was, ladies and gentlemen, and what he

was doing during that "desperate business" was singing that he was master of his fate.

If you want an example of courage try Henley. Or Stevenson. I could tell you some stories about these two, but they would not be dull enough for a rectorial address. For courage, again, take Meredith, whose laugh was "as broad as a thousand beaves at pasture." Take, as I think, the greatest figure literature has still left to us, to be added to-day to the roll of St. Andrews alumni, though it must be in absence. The pomp and circumstance of war will pass, and all others now alive may fade from the scene, but I think the quiet figure of Hardy will live on.

I seem to be taking all my examples from the calling I was lately pretending to despise. I should like to read you some passages of a letter from a man of another calling, which I think will hearten you. I have the little filmy sheets here. I thought you might like to see the actual letter; it has been a long journey; it has been to the South Pole. It is a letter to me from Captain Scott of the Antarctic, and was written in the tent you know of, where it was found long afterwards with his body and those of some other very gallant gentlemen, his comrades. The writing is in pencil, still quite clear, though toward the end some of the words trail away as into the great silence that was waiting for them. It begins: "We are pegging out in a very comfortless spot. Hoping this letter may be found and sent to you, I write you a word of farewell. I want you to think well of me and my end." [After some private instructions too intimate to read, he goes on]: "Goodbye—I am not at all afraid of the end, but sad to miss many a simple pleasure which I had planned for the future in our long marches. . . . We are in a desperate state—feet frozen, etc., no fuel, and a long way from food, but it would do your heart good to be in our tent, to hear our songs and our cheery conversation. . . . Later—[it is here that the words become difficult]—We are very near the end. . . . We did intend to finish ourselves when things proved like this, but we have decided to die naturally without."

I think it may uplift you all to stand for a moment by that tent and listen, as he says, to their songs and cheery conversation. When I think of Scott I remember the strange Alpine story of the youth who fell down a glacier and was lost, and of how a scientific companion, one of several who accompanied him, all young, computed that the body would again appear at a certain date and place many years afterwards. When

that time came round some of the survivors returned to the glacier to see if the
prediction would be fulfilled; all old men
now; and the body reappeared as young
as on the day he left them. So Scott
and his comrades emerge out of the
white immensities always young.

How comely a thing is affliction borne
cheerfully, which is not beyond the reach
of the humblest of us. What is beauty?
It is these hard-bitten men singing courage to you from their tent; it is the waves
of their island home crooning of their
deeds to you who are to follow them.
Sometimes beauty boils over and then
spirits are abroad. Ages may pass as
we look or listen, for time is annihi-
lated. There is a very old legend told
to me by Nansen the explorer—I like
well to be in the company of explorers
—the legend of a monk who had wan-
dered into the fields and a lark began to
sing. He had never heard a lark before,

and he stood there entranced until the bird and its song had become part of the heavens. Then he went back to the monastery and found there a door-keeper whom he did not know and who did not know him. Other monks came, and they were all strangers to him. He told them he was Father Anselm, but that was no help. Finally they looked through the books of the monastery, and these revealed that there had been a Father Anselm there a hundred or more years before. Time had been blotted out while he listened to the lark.

That, I suppose, was a case of beauty boiling over, or a soul boiling over; perhaps the same thing. Then spirits walk.

They must sometimes walk St. Andrews. I do not mean the ghosts of queens or prelates, but one that keeps step, as soft as snow, with some poor student. He sometimes catches sight of it. That is why his fellows can never quite touch him, their best beloved; he half knows something of which they know nothing—the secret that is hidden in the face of the Monna Lisa. As I see him, life is so beautiful to him that its proportions are monstrous. Perhaps his childhood may have been overfull of gladness; they don't like that. If the seekers were kind he is the one for whom the flags of his college would fly one day. But the seeker I am thinking of is unfriendly, and so our student is "the lad that will never be old." He often gaily forgets, and thinks he has slain his foe by daring him, like him who, dreading water, was always the first to leap into it. One can see him serene, astride a Scotch cliff, singing to the sun the farewell thanks of a boy:

"Throned on a cliff serene Man saw the sun
hold a red torch above the farthest seas,
and the fierce island pinnacles put on

In his defence their sombre panoplies;
Foremost the white mists eddied, trailed, and spun
like seekers, emulous to clasp his knees,
till all the beauty of the scene seemed one,
led by the secret whispers of the breeze.

"The sun's torch suddenly flashed upon his face
and died; and he sat content in subject night,
and dreamed of an old dead foe that had sought and found him;
a beast stirred boldly in his resting-place;
And the cold came; Man rose to his master-height,
shivered, and turned away; but the mists were round him."

If there is any of you here so rare that the seekers have taken an ill-will to him, as to the boy who wrote those lines, I ask you to be careful. Henley says in that poem we were speaking of:

"Under the bludgeonings of Chance
My head is bloody but unbowed."

A fine mouthful, but perhaps "My head is bloody and bowed" is better.

Let us get back to that tent with its songs and cheery conversation. Cour-

age. I do not think it is to be got by
your becoming solemn-sides before your
time. You must have been warned
against letting the golden hours slip by.
Yes, but some of them are golden only
because we let them slip. Diligence—
ambition; noble words, but only if
"touched to fine issues." Prizes may
be dross, learning lumber, unless they
bring you into the arena with increased
understanding. Hanker not too much
after worldly prosperity—that corpulent
cigar; if you became a millionaire you
would probably go swimming around for
more like a diseased goldfish. Look to
it that what you are doing is not merely
toddling to a competency. Perhaps that
must be your fate, but fight it and then,
though you fail, you may still be among
the elect of whom we have spoken.
Many a grave man has had to come to it
at last. But there are the complacent

toddlers from the start. Favour them
not, ladies, especially now that every one
of you carries a possible maréchal's baton
under her gown. "Happy," it has been
said by a distinguished man, "is he who
can leave college with an unreproaching
conscience and an unsullied heart." I
don't know; he sounds to me like a
sloppy, watery sort of fellow; happy,
perhaps, but if there be red blood in him
impossible. Be not disheartened by
ideals of perfection which can be
achieved only by those who run away.
Nature, that "thrifty goddess," never
gave you "the smallest scruple of her
excellence" for that. Whatever bludgeonings may be gathering for you, I think
one feels more poignantly at your age
than ever again in life. You have not
our December roses to help you; but you
have June coming, whose roses do not
wonder, as do ours even while they give

us their fragrance—wondering most when they give us most—that we should linger on an empty scene. It may indeed be monstrous but possibly courageous.

Courage is the thing. All goes if courage goes. What says our glorious Johnson of courage: "Unless a man has that virtue he has no security for preserving any other." We should thank our Creator three times daily for courage instead of for our bread, which, if we work, is surely the one thing we have a right to claim of Him. This courage is a proof of our immortality, greater even than gardens "when the eve is cool." Pray for it. "Who rises from prayer a better man, his prayer is answered." Be not merely courageous, but light-hearted and gay. There is an officer who was the first of our army to land at Gallipoli. He was dropped overboard to

[39]

light decoys on the shore, so as to deceive the Turks as to where the landing was to be. He pushed a raft containing these in front of him. It was a frosty night, and he was naked and painted black. Firing from the ships was going on all around. It was a two-hours' swim in pitch darkness. He did it, crawled through the scrub to listen to the talk of the enemy, who were so near that he could have shaken hands with them, lit his decoys and swam back. He seemed to look on this as a gay affair. He is a V. C. now, and you would not think to look at him that he could ever have presented such a disreputable appearance. Would you? (indicating Colonel Freyberg).

Those men of whom I have been speaking as the kind to fill the fife could all be light-hearted on occasion. I remember Scott by highland streams

trying to rouse me by maintaining that
haggis is boiled bagpipes; Henley in
dispute as to whether, say, Turgenieff
or Tolstoi could hang the other on
his watch-chain; he sometimes clenched
the argument by casting his crutch
at you; Stevenson responded in the
same gay spirit by giving that crutch
to John Silver; you remember with
what adequate results. You must cul-
tivate this light-heartedness if you are
to hang your betters on your watch-
chains. Dr. Johnson—let us have him
again—does not seem to have discov-
ered in his travels that the Scots are a
light-hearted nation. Boswell took him
to task for saying that the death of Garrick had eclipsed the gaiety of nations.
"Well, sir," Johnson said, "there may
be occasions when it is permissible to,"
etc. But Boswell would not let go. "I
cannot see, sir, how it could in any case

have eclipsed the gaiety of nations, as England was the only nation before whom he had ever played." Johnson was really stymied, but you would never have known it. "Well, sir," he said, holing out, "I understand that Garrick once played in Scotland, and if Scotland has any gaiety to eclipse, which, sir, I deny——"

Prove Johnson wrong for once at the Students' Union and in your other societies. I much regret that there was no Students' Union at Edinburgh in my time. I hope you are fairly noisy and that members are sometimes led out. Do you keep to the old topics? King Charles's head; and Bacon wrote Shakespeare, or if he did not he missed the opportunity of his life. Don't forget to speak scornfully of the Victorian age; there will be time for meekness when you try to better it. Very soon you will

be Victorian or that sort of thing yourselves; next session probably, when the
freshmen come up. Afterwards, if you
go in for my sort of calling, don't begin
by thinking you are the last word in art;
quite possibly you are not; steady yourselves by remembering that there were
great men before William K. Smith.
Make merry while you may. Yet light-
heartedness is not for ever and a day.
At its best it is the gay companion of
innocence; and when innocence goes—
as go it must—they soon trip off together, looking for something younger.
But courage comes all the way:

"Fight on, my men, says Sir Andrew Barton,
 I am hurt, but I am not slaine;
 I'll lie me down and bleed a-while,
 And then I'll rise and fight againe."

Another piece of advice; almost my last.
For reasons you may guess I must give
this in a low voice. Beware of M'Con-

nachie. When I look in a mirror now it is his face I see. I speak with his voice. I once had a voice of my own, but nowadays I hear it from far away only, a melancholy, lonely, lost little pipe. I wanted to be an explorer, but he willed otherwise. You will all have your M'Connachies luring you off the high road. Unless you are constantly on the watch, you will find that he has slowly pushed you out of yourself and taken your place. He has rather done for me. I think in his youth he must somehow have guessed the future and been fleggit by it, flichtered from the nest like a bird, and so our eggs were left, cold. He has clung to me, less from mischief than for companionship; I half like him and his penny whistle; with all his faults he is as Scotch as peat; he whispered to me just now that you elected him, not me, as your Rector.

A final passing thought. Were an old
student given an hour in which to re-
visit the St. Andrews of his day, would
he spend more than half of it at lec-
tures? He is more likely to be heard
clattering up bare stairs in search of old
companions. But if you could choose
your hour from all the five hundred
years of this seat of learning, wandering
at your will from one age to another,
how would you spend it? A fascinating
theme; so many notable shades at once
astir that St. Leonard's and St. Mary's
grow murky with them. Hamilton,
Melville, Sharpe, Chalmers, down to
Herkless, that distinguished Principal,
ripe scholar and warm friend, the loss of
whom I deeply deplore with you. I
think if that hour were mine, and though
at St. Andrews he was but a passer-by,
I would give a handsome part of it to a
walk with Dr. Johnson. I should like
to have the time of day passed to me in

twelve languages by the Admirable Crichton. A wave of the hand to Andrew Lang; and then for the archery butts with the gay Montrose, all a-ruffled and ringed, and in the gallant St. Andrews student manner, continued as I understand, to this present day, scattering largess as he rides along,

> "But where is now the courtly troupe
>   That once went riding by?
> I miss the curls of Canteloupe,
>   The laugh of Lady Di."

We have still left time for a visit to a house in South Street, hard by St. Leonard's. I do not mean the house you mean. I am a Knox man. But little will that avail, for M'Connachie is a Queen Mary man. So, after all, it is at her door we chap, a last futile effort to bring that woman to heel. One more house of call, a student's room, also in South Street. I have chosen my student,

you see, and I have chosen well; him
that sang—

> "Life has not since been wholly vain,
>   And now I bear
> Of wisdom plucked from joy and pain
>   Some slender share.

> "But howsoever rich the store,
>   I'd lay It down
> To feel upon my back once more
>   The old red gown."

Well, we have at last come to an end.
Some of you may remember when I began this address; we are all older now.
I thank you for your patience. This is
my first and last public appearance, and
I never could or would have made it
except to a gathering of Scottish students. If I have concealed my emotions
in addressing you it is only the thrawn
national way that deceives everybody
except Scotsmen. I have not been as
dull as I could have wished to be; but
looking at your glowing faces cheerful-

ness and hope would keep breaking through. Despite the imperfections of your betters we leave you a great inheritance, for which others will one day call you to account. You come of a race of men the very wind of whose name has swept to the ultimate seas. Remember—

"Heaven doth with us as we with torches do,
  Not light them for themselves. . . ."

Mighty are the Universities of Scotland, and they will prevail. But even in your highest exultations never forget that they are not four, but five. The greatest of them is the poor, proud homes you come out of, which said so long ago: "There shall be education in this land." She, not St. Andrews, is the oldest university in Scotland, and all the others are her whelps.

In bidding you good-bye, my last words must be of the lovely virtue.

COURAGE

Courage, my children, and "greet the unseen with a cheer." "Fight on, my men," said Sir Andrew Barton. Fight on—you—for the old red gown till the whistle blows.